HEALTHY MONEY

Making a Successful Transition
from Resident to Attending

Written By

John W. Crane, CLU®, ChFC®, RICP®, MBA

http://www.cranefinancial.com

ISBN-13: 978-0692934173 (Healthy Money)
ISBN-10: 0692934170

INVITE JOHN TO SPEAK
TO YOUR GROUP

John is a regular speaker at local area hospitals in the Washington, DC Metro Area on personal finance topics related to physicians. If you would like to have John speak at your event, please contact his offices at 703-635-3300 or submit your request at http://www.cranefinancial.com/contact.

TABLE OF CONTENTS

NOTE TO THE READER

INTRODUCTION

NOTE TO THE READER

This book was written for you, **to share with you what I've learned about helping our Nations Healers make the topic of money a positive in their lives.**

I want this book to have utility and to be helpful. I know some of you will read the entire book from cover to cover. Others of you will leaf through it as fast as possible to see if they can find the nuggets that will be of most value to them.

~~~~~~~~

For those of you that aren't interested in reading this book and instead just want an outline to look through, please turn to the back of the book and <u>on pages 105 through 114 you will find a summary of the Action Steps contained throughout the book</u>.

ACKNOWLEDGEMENTS

First and foremost, I wish to thank my wife Linda and my daughter Emma. You both make my everyday life **great**. I am thankful for how supportive you were of me taking on this book project.

I'd also like to thank Dr. Jeffrey Berger at George Washington University Hospital. When we met back in 2009, we began collaborating on the best way to share financial education to the residents without making it sound like a financial product push. Dr. Berger continues to be generous with his time in being a sounding board as I work to make my presentations better and more valuable to the physicians.

A special thank you to Dr. Tamara Hayes who originally introduced me to Dr. Berger.

Writing is something that I've always enjoyed and the roots of that enjoyment came from my English Teachers at Byram Hills High School. Thank you to Mr. Jock Montgomery, Mr. Robert Shapiro (sophomore and junior year) and Mr. J. Allan Pryor.

ABOUT THE AUTHOR

John W. Crane, CLU®, ChFC®, RICP®, MBA is a financial advisor with more than a decade of experience in the financial services industry. He has devoted his career to providing financial guidance to business professionals, corporate executives of small and mid-sized businesses, and medical specialists. Familiar with the many life events and career milestones these clients face over the years, he utilizes a vision discussion and a comprehensive planning process to identify each client's unique goals and financial picture. Only once he understands their circumstances and needs does he work on creating a financial strategy designed to help them budget, protect what's important, build their wealth, and achieve financial balance. He is passionate about the opportunities his career offers to make a difference in people's lives. He seeks to be the first person his clients call when they receive big news, whether good or bad, serving as a constant and an advocate in their lives.

John believes extensive financial education is the cornerstone for a strong advisor. He holds FINRA Series 7, 63, and 65 securities registrations and his life and health insurance licenses. As a Chartered Life Underwriter® and a Chartered Financial Consultant®, he has advanced knowledge and experience in the financial planning, investment management, and insurance fields. He received a Bachelor of Science in Marketing Management from

Susquehanna University and a Master of Business Administration from George Mason University.

John's commitment to education extends beyond his own credentials. He frequently presents to graduating resident fellows at George Washington University Hospital regarding financial planning. He is also a guest speaker at T.C. Williams High School, speaking to the Academy of Finance students about career planning, financial planning, and other topics.

John lives in Alexandria, Virginia with his wife, Linda, and their daughter, Emma. When he isn't spending time with his family and attending Emma's sports games, he enjoys staying active. Along with cycling, he enjoys running and completed a few marathons including the New York City Marathon in 2014.

~~~~~~~~~

To learn more about John or to access further resources, please visit here:

Website: http://www.cranefinancial.com
Blog: http://www.cranefinancial.com/blog
Follow On Facebook: CraneFinancialAlexandria
LinkedIN: https://www.linkedin.com/in/johncrane/

HEALTHY MONEY

Making a Successful Transition from Resident to Attending

INTRODUCTION

Mary sat down with a heavy sigh and leaned her head against the wall. She closed her eyes and started to massage her temples, hoping against hope the pounding in her head would abate for a few minutes.

"You all right?" her roommate's voice came out of nowhere, startling her.

She pried her eyes open with a groan, "I've been better."

"Tough day?" Jennifer asked.

Mary snorted. "Tough year." It had, in fact, been a tough few years, ever since she started her residency. She loved being a doctor and being able to help people. In fact, it had been her dream since she was a little girl. However, as far as she could remember, her dream never included the grueling hours or ridiculous workload of being a resident.

"Tell me about it. I can barely keep my eyes open and I feel like I've been run over by a truck. When we get home, I'm going to fall into bed and sleep for a week."

"Oh, if only we could…"

Jennifer sighed. "Yeah, but it's a good dream as dreams go. Anyway, it's no use whining about it. It's not as if we have much of a choice."

"We do have a choice," Mary pointed out. "We could quit."

Her roommate gave her a horrified look. "Please tell me you're kidding. Now, when we've only got one year left? Are you insane?"

Mary looked at her friend with tired eyes. "I don't know if I am... I must be, though. I guess I'm just tired and feeling a little overwhelmed." The fact of the matter was that she was really tired. She was tired of sharing an apartment that was the size of a matchbox, she was tired of working like a slave for about as much money, she was tired of being up to her eyeballs in debt, and she was tired of not having a social life.

"Are you okay?"

"It's my birthday tomorrow," Mary replied. "I'll be 27 and my greatest accomplishment is the mountain of debt on my back that I haven't been able to even touch. Shouldn't things be easier?"

"Hey, come on, things aren't that bad. I mean, look how far you've come. You're one year away from being an attending physician and then money won't be an issue anymore."

"Sometimes I wonder. I mean, I obviously have the financial acumen of a lobotomized penguin."

Jennifer burst out laughing, "That's a good one. Though, really, you shouldn't feel special. I'm pretty sure being terrible with finances is a prerequisite for becoming a doctor. You know I come from a family of doctors and all I can say is that I'm glad my parents decided to get professional financial advice, or I'd have grown up eating beans on toast."

Mary gave her skeptical look. "Don't give me that. Remember, we spent Thanksgiving together with your folks. I've seen where you grew up. It's a castle."

"Yeah, it is. But one reason they have that place is because they got professional advice on managing their finances," Jennifer explained. "Just look at my brother. Liam's been an attending for almost 4 years now, and he's in worse financial shape than I am. And I earn a fifth of what he does. He just refuses to listen to mom and dad and thinks he knows it all. I hope he wakes up and realizes the mistake he's making before it's too late."

"Professional financial advice? Never thought of that." And Mary really hadn't. In fact, she hadn't even realized that there was such a thing.

"Well, think about it. We're doctors, right? People come to us when they are not well because we're the experts. So, doesn't it make sense for us to seek the advice of experts when we have problems?"

"Yeah, I guess you're right. But if you're so gung ho on this idea, why haven't you gotten financial advice yet?"

"Well, I kind of have. My parents' financial advisor gives me advice now and then. He only really works with attendings, but he's been working with my parents for so long that it's almost like he's part of the family. So, he's been giving me some pointers, and I'll definitely be signing up with him once I've finished my residency. I really, really do not want to end up like my brother."

Mary looked at her roommate thoughtfully. Jennifer always did seem so put together and well organized. And, she'd never been late with the rent, nor had Mary ever seen her resort to noodles because she'd run out of money for food, as happened to her quite often. In fact, Jennifer always seemed to be able to go out for meals with friends and even go away for a weekend, every now and then. Mary had always thought it was because Jennifer's parents were helping her out. After all, they were both doctors, whereas Mary's parents were blue-collar workers.

"Don't your parents help you out with money?" Mary blurted out and then blushed with embarrassment. "Sorry, I shouldn't have asked that. It's none of my business."

Jennifer chuckled. "Don't worry about it. And no, my parents don't help me with money. They didn't even help me pay for college or med school. They're of the philosophy that I have to prove I can stand on my own two feet first. They both come from pretty poor backgrounds and have always maintained that the if they could succeed, so should we. My brother really resents them for it, and I did too at one point. Now, though, I'm actually glad for it."

"So, basically, you're telling me that the main reason you're not living on stale bread, like some of us, is because of your parents' financial advisor and not because your parents give you money, right?"

Mary looked up at Jennifer's founding countenance and rushed to reassure her, "I need to understand because I really need help. I feel like I'm running around like a chicken without a head and, no matter what I do, I can't seem to get ahead. But I thought that was the way it was for anyone during their residency when they don't have external financial support."

Jennifer shook her head. "Yeah, a lot of our colleagues are in the same boat, but they don't have to be. And neither do you. How about we go home, get some dinner, and we can start working through your finances. I'll help you out with the advice I have gotten over the years and hopefully, things will start looking better for you soon."

"If you could help me, that would be amazing. It would definitely make my life a lot easier if I didn't have to worry about finances."

~~~~~~~~~~~

Mary's situation is a pretty common one among residents. Years of schooling and training, grueling work hours for relatively little pay, and ridiculously high expenses mean that most residents aren't in the best of financial shape.

As a resident, you probably have a lot in common with Mary and you know exactly how draining it is to have to worry about your finances on top of all the responsibilities associated with the residency program you're going through. Sometimes, you probably just want to stick your head in the sand and ignore your financial situation completely because it comes much too overwhelming to deal with.

The good news is that I can help you and that's why I have written this book. Don't worry, I have no intention of trying to teach you everything about finances. And I'm definitely not going to bore you to tears. My goal is to help you through a tough time with simple but effective tips and advice.

We will be following Mary's story throughout the book and you'll be able to see how things change for her as she finally takes control of her finances, instead of allowing her finances to control her. Yes, Mary is fiction, but she represents a culmination of virtually every resident I've worked with in the past. I now mainly work with attendings, but I know how important it is to get a head start with your finances. If you take control now, while you're still a resident, you'll be able to achieve that and much more once you become an attending.

Before we continue with Mary's story, though, like to tell you a different story. My story. After all, if we're going to be working together within the pages of this book, we have to get to know each other. So, here's the story of how I discovered my passion and became a financial advisor.

SECTION I

A NEW CAREER

SECTION I: A NEW CAREER

When I was 30 years old, I became the youngest Senior National Account Manager at Sprint. I was assigned to their largest account, the Department of Veterans Affairs. I was already married to my wife Linda, owned my own home, drove a nice car, just finished my Masters in Business Administration degree, and my annual salary was over $150,000.

By all external measures, I had won the game of life in Corporate America. According to 'the rules', I was a success because I had everything I had worked for, had wanted, or had been told to want.

The problem was that I wasn't truly happy. For a number of years, a feeling of discontent had been growing inside of me, but I kept pushing it aside. I kept telling myself that I could tolerate pretty much anything for the right amount of money.

In the world of business-to-business sales and account management, ideally, when you take over a sales territory the previous account manager is still there to "train" you. This usually means he walks you into each account contact, introduces you and vouches for you to their account contact. That was the exact situation I walked into with my new job.

The person that I was taking over for was named Tom. He was 65-years old and retiring after managing his sales territory for the past 10 years. Truly an awesome guy all around, great family man and a Navy Veteran. I learned a lot from him during our time together.

When taking over a territory, the situation doesn't get much better than what I was walking into. My first two months on the job overlapped with his last two months. We traveled together down the East Coast as he introduced me to all the key contacts and decision makers, and explained all of the sales opportunities.

On one of these trips, we were in Tuscaloosa, AL eating breakfast at a Waffle House. While we were sitting together in a booth and Tom was telling me about who we were going to meet that day, all of a sudden, a big truth hit me.

'I don't really care about what he's talking about or what I am about to do today,' I thought. Of course, I cared in the sense that I wanted to do a good job. Otherwise, though, I had little interest in large data networks and the electronics that made them work.

Suddenly, an even bigger truth hit me as the reality of my life situation became clear. A rushing sound filled my ears and I couldn't even hear Tom anymore. I looked down at the table, then across it and, finally, up at Tom.

'I'm 30-years old. Tom is 65-years old. The chronological distance between my side of the table and his side of the table is 35-years. At this point, 35-years was longer than I had been alive. I had more than a lifetime to go and I didn't like my job,' I thought. Panic started to set in as what I had previously considered to be a great job opportunity morphed into what now felt like a death sentence.

The waitress asked us if we wanted more coffee. Tom was still talking about the account contact. Neither of them were aware of my turmoil. Tom certainly had no clue that his successor across the table was experiencing a moment of crisis.

I knew then that I had to get off the track that I was on and reinvent myself. I needed a new career. Sprint was a good company and the job that I had fought for was a good job. It was a good opportunity for somebody — somebody else.

My break down at the Waffle House led to a year of self-discovery. Using multiple yellow pads and notebooks I wrote down my likes, dislikes, and attributes of my ideal job. I recorded my best habits and worked hard to learn who I really was. I used that image to find the profession suited me best. As this image started to take shape, I'd interview people that knew me well and ask them if they could see me doing this job or that job. The career role that got the most positive feedback was financial advisor. Not only could my friends see me doing it, they told me that if I took that route to let them know because they wanted to hire me.

Fifteen months later, I drove out of the Sprint parking lot for the last time and started my new career in the financial services industry.

MY FIRST FORAY INTO THE WORLD OF FINANCIAL ADVICE

Finding a good firm to launch my career was a challenge for me. I didn't know a lot about how the industry worked or about the players in the industry. They all looked the same to me. I interviewed at all of the big investment houses – the names you'd recognize from the commercials that run during football games on Sunday's or the ads you see while sitting on metro trains. My interviews at all these different companies took a similar path. I'd ask all of the questions that one would ask when interviewing for a job. Selfishly, I had one key question that was the essence of each interview.

"OK, a prospective client walks into your office carrying this huge stack of financial stuff. They give it to you. You read it and make recommendations, right?" I'd ask.

The advisor would look at me a little annoyed, "Yes, that is what we do here".

I continued, "Great. So, what do you base your advice and recommendations on?"

The answers I was getting weren't good answers. Instead of a clear methodology or client-based advice, the advice generally gravitated towards pushing the financial products the firm sold.

I was frustrated so I reached out to a friend of mine from college whose father owned a financial firm in Baltimore, MD. The daily drive would have been too long so I hadn't initially considered the firm as a potential place to work, which was why I hadn't reached out in the first place. By this time, I was extremely frustrated and no longer had a lot of faith. I needed a friendly face to explain the industry to me.

We met for lunch near his office and he broke the industry down for me, which is essentially made up of investment companies (wire houses), insurance companies and fee-only financial planning firms. All the places I had talked to were investment companies. His firm was insurance based and they also managed investments for their clients. With his help, I had a better handle on the industry and why I was hearing what I was hearing. I took a deep breath and asked him my big question.

"When your advisors give advice to their clients, what is that advice based on?" To be honest, by this point I was completely certain I'd be disappointed in his answer.

Without hesitation, he replied, "We use a planning process based on a series of financial tutorials that cover everything from your personal insurances, your insurances through work, cash savings, investments, real estate, debt management and cash flow management."

He then shifted gears and told me that he had recently acquired a firm in the Washington, DC metro area closer to where I lived.

"John, I'd like to suggest you meet with the person that runs our Washington, DC office. Let us do your plan. See it for yourself through the eyes of a prospective client. Then, you'll be able to see if its what you are looking for."

Two weeks later, I met with an advisor in their Washington, DC office to start going through the planning process. After I went through all their tutorials, this advisor proved to me that this firm had a methodology they followed to educate the client on the who, what, where, when, why and how behind their recommendations. I made the decision to join this firm and started immediately.

WHY I DECIDED TO SPECIALIZE IN WORKING WITH PHYSICIANS

There are a lot of financial advisors out there, many of whom are excellent and really do care about their clients. But, there aren't quite as many who understand exactly what you, as a resident transitioning to an attending, are going through right now.

Physicians are unique individuals with unique needs. You have to be incredibly smart and talented to become a physician. If you aren't smart, you cannot possibly learn all the things you need to know to graduate from medical school and to get selected into a good residency program. If you aren't talented, you cannot possibly execute on your craft in a manner that will allow you to graduate residency. And if you're not executing, it won't be any fun for you – you might even quit before they throw you out.

So, not only are you beyond smart and talented, but you're also expected to work pretty hard for very little compensation, at least at first. You're dealing with massive loans and expenses, and all the bills just keep piling up while you're eating noodles and even at times maybe wondering why you're even bothering.

And then, you come to the end of your residency and are staring at a contract with a massive amount of money on it. Life's going to be so different, right? After all, you're not earning a pittance anymore. But soon enough, you realize all the financial baggage you brought with you from your school days and residency is acting like a millstone around your neck and seems to be dragging you deeper and deeper into the muck.

When I say financial baggage, I'm not referring just to the debt, but also to the bad financial habits you've picked up along the way. It's understandable. You were studying to be a doctor and now you're focused on saving people's lives. No one can expect you to be a financial wizard too. But, it's hurting you and causing more stress than you need in an already stressful life. And these are issues you shouldn't be facing – certainly not alone – when you are such a smart, talented, unique individual who has dedicated their life to helping other people.

That's precisely why I ended up specializing in working with attending physicians. Just like you have the knowledge and skills to help people and do so every day, I have the knowledge and skills to help you.

The story of how I came to work with resident and attending physicians is pretty simple. In 2009, I was referred to a resident physician that was in her final year of training. They are a wonderful family. With the student loans and the low income that residents are paid, their finances were under stress. She explained to me that she was about to sign a contract where her income was going to increase five-fold.

It was then that I also saw that this was an inflection point in the life of this family. A properly executed cash flow strategy could potentially remove the financial stress from their lives – forever.

I began interviewing resident and attending physicians. Anyone that I could get to talk to me I'd go an interview them. I wanted to know how the training years (residency and fellowship) worked. I wanted to know how one became an attending physician. I wanted to know how their loans worked. I wanted to know and understand everything because I'd finally found the place where I could be of use. Where I could make a difference.

That's my story. Now, you know who I am and why I'm uniquely qualified to help you with your finances. So, let's get back to Mary's story and discover how she shed the millstone from around her neck.

SECTION II

PROTECTION MATTERS

SECTION II: PROTECTION MATTERS

Mary could feel the panic bubbling up at her chest and the commotion in the ER did nothing to stem the tide of anxiety that was threatening to overtake her. She didn't know why she was reacting this way. It wasn't her first rotation in the ER, nor was it the first time she'd seen the results of a car wreck. Then again, it was her first 20 car pile up. And she had been on her feet for 12 hours already. She had in getting ready to end her shift when the call came in and it was all hands on deck.

Everywhere she looked, people were in pain. She grimaced as she looked at some of the incoming patients. Not everyone was going to walk away from the situation intact. In fact, she was pretty certain quite a few people would not be walking away at all, though she and her colleagues would do everything in their power to help them. But sometimes, the matter how hard you tried, there was nothing you could do. And those were the most difficult times.

The people who would be walking away with disabilities would have their lives turned upside down. Jennifer had tried to explain to her the importance of protection, but Mary was ashamed to admit she had really paid attention. All she'd heard was that it would be an additional cost – one which she felt she couldn't afford at the moment – so, her brain and shut down. After all, the chance of something happening to her was minimal.

As she looked around the ER, though, she realized that everyone there had probably thought the same thing. She couldn't help but wonder if any of them had any form of protection in place. It started to click in her mind that they wouldn't be the only ones to suffer. In fact, their families would suffer just as much, if not more so.

She imagined herself in that position and wondered what would happen to her if she lost the ability to work. Her parents would have to look after her, which would make their lives so much harder. And what would happen to her debt? She still have to pay it off. But with what? And how would your parents care for her? They didn't make enough money to take care of someone who was disabled. And they are close to retirement age. But they wouldn't give up on her. They tried their best would probably mean working longer hours and pushing their retirement forward, just because she hadn't been bothered to think about the future.

No, she wouldn't do that to her parents or herself. She'd asked Jennifer to explain everything to her again and this time, she would not only pay attention but also commit to do something about it. Decision made, Mary felt better as the sense of reasserting her control infused her with more confidence. She drew herself up, pushed the panic down and went into doctor mode, i.e. completely focused on the people that needed her skills.

Later that evening, she sat down with Jennifer. "I'm sorry. I should have listened to you. You were right and today's accident was a serious wake-up call. So, can you please explain the entire protection thing again?"

"Okay, I'll do my best. I've got my notes this time, so maybe I'll be better able to explain it to you, just like my parents financial advisor explained it to me. In fact, he drilled the importance of protection into my head so well that it's now completely ingrained. And, every time I see someone suffer a stroke or heart attack or end up in a car wreck, I thank him for pushing me to get protection so that my future will be taken care of if something does happen."

Mary nodded. "It has been a long time since I panicked in the ER but seeing all those people and realizing that many of them might not be able to work again hit me really hard. It really drove the point home of how naïve and childish I've been acting. So, let me have it. I'm all ears."

"So, this is the way I parents financial advisor explained the importance of protection to me:

Imagine you are driving home on a Friday afternoon and it is the start of a long holiday weekend. You just completed your first month as an attending physician. Good music is playing on the radio to accompany you as you navigate light traffic on the way home. You approach the next intersection and the light is green. As you pass through the intersection, a distracted driver misses his red light and slams into the driver side door of your car. You black out.

Eventually, you wake up in a hospital bed surrounded by your colleagues. The ambulance took you to the nearest hospital, which is where you are completing your medical training. After working with you for a few days, the specialists determine that the injuries from the accident are sufficient to exclude you from the world of work. You are permanently disabled.

Obviously, there is physical and emotional pain to work through. Once you've made your initial progress there, you need to start thinking about what has been taken away from you. In addition to the physical losses, you've also suffered pretty significant financial losses as a result of your permanent disability.

"Okay, that last bit sounded a bit like French. Physical losses, financial losses?" Mary was sure her confusion showed on her face.

"Well, physical losses pretty much mean the results of the injuries you suffered. So, for example, if you're paralyzed, you can't get back the use of your legs. And financial losses refer to the money you've lost as a result of the accident, namely the income you will no longer be earning because you can't work. Make sense?"

"Now it does. Go on."

There is an economic measure of the value of a human being's lifetime of future earnings called Human Life Value. A 30-year old, brand new attending physician has a full career worth of wages in their future. We can use Human Life Value (HLV) to consider what that loss might look like in terms of a present day lump sum of money. That lump sum (HLV) may be defined as the capitalized monetary worth of a wage earners future earnings taking into account their education, experience and their chosen career field backing out inflation, taxes and personal consumption.[i] For the purposes of our discussion here, one can estimate their Human Life Value as a multiple of their current gross income depending on your age. The rough rule of thumb in the life insurance and disability insurance industries[ii] is as follows:

- In your 20s, it is 20x to 30x gross income
- In your 30s, it is 20x gross income
- In your 40s, it is 15x gross income
- In your 50s, it is 10x gross income

HOW TO CALCULATE YOUR HLV

> **My Starting Annual Attending Salary:** _____
>
> **X**
>
> **Multiplier from above table** _____
>
> **=**
>
> **My Human Life Value** _____

Imagine the person that hit you was extremely wealthy and just felt horrible about the accident. They cannot eat or sleep because they are completely wracked with guilt. They come to your home and present you with a check for your Human Life Value.

Picture this scene in your mind: the present value of all your future earnings is in your possession. You are now at home and sitting on your couch, recovering from your injuries. You have the check deposited in your checking account and are looking at the account balance on your smartphone. As you look at the balance, you realize that, while you have the funds in your account, you are still permanently disabled and will never be able to work again.

Consider this question:

You are now a multimillionaire. Do you feel like you are wealthy? Yes / No. Why or why not?" Jennifer paused in her explanation, looking at Mary expectantly.

"Oh, you want me to answer. Okay. Well, I guess I'd be wealthy…" Mary trailed off, watching Jennifer's expression. "Or not?"

"Well, why do you feel you'd be wealthy?" Jennifer persisted, obviously trying not to give the answer away.

"If I work out my HLV now, as a resident, with my current paycheck, I'd get between $1.1 million and $1.65 million. That's a lot of money," Mary replied, her eyes glazing over at what she could do with that amount of money.

"True but you have to be honest and ask yourself how long would it last you, for real? I mean, you're barely making ends meet now, and you don't have all the additional costs associated with being disabled. The medical costs alone will suck up a lot of that. But, it's definitely better than not having any income at all."

"So, what are you saying? That all this HLV stuff is a waste of time?" Mary asked, perplexed.

"Far from it. What I'm saying is that you won't be wealthy. You'll just have the money you need to get by if something happens to you now, but it's definitely better than nothing. You also want to put it to work for you, but we'll talk about that some other time. This leads into the next point I want to make.

Consider the following paradigm: Imagine that instead of having your car accident now, you had your car accident after being an attending physician for five years. Would your annual income be less, more or the same? Most likely it will be more because you are more established and a better physician at that point. Using an estimate of an attending salary 5 years into your career, recalculate the estimate of your Human Life Value. Is it more than your original estimate?" Once again, Jennifer paused, waiting for an answer.

"Well, yeah, since I'm hoping I'll be making at least around $300,000, so my HLV would be between $6 million and $9 million…" Mary trailed off, realizing just how gigantic those amounts seemed. She couldn't even imagine what that kind of money looked like.

"Right. So, if something happens to you now, your financial loss will be approximately $1.65 million but if something happens to you in five years' time, then your financial loss could be valued at closer to $9 million. That's because the Human Life Value calculation establishes a dollar amount based upon who you are in the world today, not necessarily on who you will become later on down the road. Further, the dollar amount is designed to be the net present value of all your future paychecks backing out inflation and taxes. It is designed to put you in the same financial position as if you were healthy and earning all of those paychecks through retirement age. Understand?"

Mary nodded. "I get it. So, I can expect my HLV to be calculated based on the amount I'm earning when something happens to and it doesn't always take into account how much I could have earned if I'd been able to continue in my career."

Jennifer nodded. "Exactly."

"Doesn't seem fair, does it?"

"Well, yes and no. Remember, no two people are alike and it would be impossible to determine how far ahead you'd be able to get in your career. No one has a crystal ball to be able to tell the future."

"I guess you're right. And it's definitely a lot better than having no income at all, right?"

"Exactly. Now, we're going to shift gears a little. Imagine that you were not the victim of this accident, rather you were the one who ran the red light and caused the accident. The person you hit happens to be one of your colleagues, so they have the same Human Life Value calculation result. There is a chance that they might consider a lawsuit to recover their Human Life Value.

You may want to consider obtaining Umbrella Liability Insurance coverage to help protect your current and future finances from losses stemming from an accident of this nature. Talk to whomever you currently have your car insurance through and ask them to explain how Umbrella Liability Insurance works in the context of Human Life Value and the accident examples that we discussed. They are the experts and will be able to provide you with the guidance you'll need.

~~~~~~~~~~~

YOU CAN NEVER GET PROTECTION TOO EARLY

Mary is lucky that she's learning about protection now before something happens to her. Unfortunately, many residents don't discover how much they're risking until it's too late. And, in fact, this applies to any industry. I learned about the importance of protection when I first went up to Washington DC as part of the series of tutorials the firm conducted. It made a large impact on me.

I could clearly see that when the paycheck stopped permanently there was a subsequent financial loss. Up until that point in my life, I had worked in Corporate America and, every two weeks, a paycheck showed up in my checking account. It never really occurred to me that a scenario might come about where that might stop. Some of that is tied to being a young man, as we believe we are invincible, but mostly it was because I am an optimist and tend to focus on positive things.

The advisor highlighted my Human Life Value, which set at $3,000,000 at the time. So, he explained that if I became permanently disabled in a car accident, the loss of my future paychecks was valued at $3,000,000.

Then he asked me, "What if you became permanently disabled, but it was due to a health issue like a stroke? What is the value of your lost paychecks then?"

"My paychecks have permanently stopped, so I guess it's still $3,000,000," I answered.

"What if you died in your sleep due to a health issue? What is the value of your lost paychecks then?"

Trying to inject some levity into a very morbid conversation, "Well, I don't know anybody that still goes to work after becoming dead, so I guess it's still $3,000,000," I answered.

The advisor confirmed my answers. "Yes, it doesn't really matter HOW your paychecks permanently stop from the standpoint of measuring the loss to your family and your Balance Sheet. The difference is how you deal with the loss in terms of the insurance coverage that you have in place."

My eyes drifted to the summary of my current coverage for auto insurance, long-term disability insurance, and life insurance. The insurance I had in place covered less than 10% of my Human Life Value. Any event leading to a permanent loss of income would create a huge burden on my family. I took the necessary actions to fix the situation.

BECOMING A FINANCIAL ADVISOR

When you start in the financial services industry, you are typically handed a document called a 'Project 100'. This document is where you are to record the 100 people that you know best and this will act as a starting point for acquiring clients. Since you are brand new and have no knowledge, you are teamed with a senior advisor and they help train you while you add your first wave of clients. Once you've reached a level of mastery, the senior advisor is no longer involved and you serve clients on your own. My original 'Project 100' included my first 12 clients. These original clients helped introduce me to other potential clients and my practice began to grow. The process of reinventing myself into a financial advisor was well underway.

Two years later, it was a real hot day in August and I was mowing my lawn. My phone vibrated, indicating an incoming call, so I turned off the mower and took the call.

"Hey, John. It's Steve." Steve was a good friend and happened to also be one of my original 12 clients.

"John, I don't know how to tell you this, but Daniel died this morning. Without any warning, he just dropped to the floor and his heart stopped."

This would be shocking news under any circumstances, but especially shocking in this case. Steve, Daniel and I had all worked at Sprint together. He was in his early 30s, in good health and had run a marathon in the past couple of years. Out of anyone, Daniel wasn't supposed to die.

In the coming week, we all met for the funeral. It was a very sad time for all of us as we missed our friend and we struggled with the confusion of how someone so young and healthy could just pass on without warning. It just did not make any sense whatsoever.

My role in all of this was not complete. A few weeks after the funeral, I met with Daniel's wife and handed her a check for $2,000,000. That was Daniel's Human Life Value.

Steve had recommended to Daniel that he work with me as his financial advisor, so he'd become my client.

Once I had delivered the check, I felt like I had done something great that had given my very short career tremendous meaning. But I was also tortured by the thought that for me to get to this point, my friend Daniel had died. How could I feel good about this? It took me many years to process that conflict.

That experience created a conviction in me that is unshakable. Through this experience, I watched a $2,000,000 life insurance policy turn into $2,000,000 of cash in a checking account. The insurance definitely works and it is definitely the right amount. Upon receiving the check, the first words out of my client's mouth were, "You know, $2,000,000 sounds like a lot of money, but it really is not. It just replaces his annual paycheck." She, more than anyone, got it.

WHAT SHOULD MARY DO?

The first thing Mary needs to do is to look into Umbrella Liability Insurance, long-term disability protection and life insurance. Let's take a closer look at each of these and how they can help Mary in the long run.

~~~~~~~~~~

UMBRELLA LIABILITY INSURANCE

Umbrella Insurance is invaluable because it may help protect your income and your assets in the event of a lawsuit. Most people don't realize how important this protection is until it's too late and they are faced with having to sell off everything they ever worked for because of a silly mistake. The sad fact is that we live in a litigious society – i.e. everyone is lawsuit happy – and you never know what could lead to someone filing a lawsuit against you.

Whatever you do, don't fall into the "this will never happen to me" trap. It's almost a self-fulfilling prophecy – being uninsured or under-insured seems to attract trouble like bees to honey.

Contact your Property and Casualty Agent today and inquire about Umbrella Liability Insurance and how it may help protect your assets and future income.

LONG-TERM DISABILITY INSURANCE

Long-term disability protection is vital if you want to avoid future catastrophes. This type of protection ensures you will still receive an income while you are unable to work due to an accident or because of illness.

I can't stress enough how important it is to get long-term disability protection as soon as possible. The younger you are, the better. You might be tempted to wait until you finish your residency, but this is a mistake. Right now, you are as young and as healthy as you'll ever be and your premiums are calculated according to how healthy you are and your age. You'll never get cheaper premiums than right now.

And if you think you'll never need long-term disability protection, you couldn't be further from the facts of life. The Social Security Administration has stated that approximately 25% of 20-year-olds will lose their ability to work because of a disability before they reach the age of 67[iii].That's one in 4.

So, yes, you might be one of the lucky ones, but do you really want to take that chance? Remember, this is your life we're talking about. If the worst happens and you don't have coverage, you are going to end up broke with no way to look after yourself and you'll become a financial drain on your family.

It's vital that you protect your unique ability and you don't end up in a situation where you are basically the walking dead. Being disabled is difficult enough, especially when it's so serious that you can't work, and the last thing you need to compound that situation with is financial problems.

When shopping around for long-term disability insurance, you should first try to find a licensed agent that really knows what they're talking about, and has experience working with healthcare professionals. And, like with any product, you get what you pay for, so get as much coverage as you can possibly afford right now, even if it means cutting back on other things.

You might be tempted to delay the decision, but you are risking a lot by doing so. In my career, I've worked with a few clients that decided to wait until they finished the residency to purchase a long-term disability policy. In the meantime, they developed health problems and were no longer able to get a good deal on their long-term disability insurance contracts.

LIFE INSURANCE

Life insurance offers a number of benefits, of which the most important life coverage. Essentially, this means that the person you appoint as beneficiary will receive a certain amount of money if you pass away while the policy is still active. In other words, a life insurance policy will make sure that the future of the people you love is financially secure, even if you are no longer around.

Life insurance is definitely important, but if you have to choose between long-term disability protection life insurance, at this stage I typically advise physicians who are single without any dependents to opt for long-term disability protection over life insurance. This is because if you become disabled and cannot work, you are still alive and have expenses that need to be covered, yet you are not earning any income. If you pass away, you will no longer be incurring any expenses.

On the other hand, if you have a spouse and/or children, then you may want to consider trying to strike a balance between the two, so you can at least protect the immediate financial future of your family, regardless of whether you are no longer able to create income due to death or disability.

SECTON II: ACTION ITEMS

1) **UMBRELLA LIABILITY INSURANCE**: Take the previously outlined scenario to your auto insurance and homeowner's insurance agent and ask them how you can protect yourself from personal lawsuit.

2) **LONG-TERM DISABILITY PROTECTION**: You have to protect your unique ability (your specific specialty) because the last thing you want to do is end up being the living dead. You might be tempted to pick up the first insurance policy you find, but you will have to work with a licensed agent that has deep knowledge in this area or you are short-changing yourself. Remember, you get what you pay for, and cutting corners might save you a buck or two in the short-term, but could lead you and your family to financial ruin in the long term.

I'm pretty sure you're thinking that you don't need to worry about long-term disability protection now. It's too early. You're too young.

Well, try this. Walk over to a mirror and take a good look. As you are admiring the view, know this: You are as young and healthy as we are ever going to be in this present moment. It doesn't get any better than this right now. I've had two clients that decided to wait until they completed residency and during that small window experienced adverse changes to their health that precluded them from getting good long-term disability insurance contracts. Everyone needs to make the decision on how and when to get coverage that suits them best, however please recognize that delaying the decision isn't without risk.

So, find a good agent who is intimately acquainted and has extensive experience in working with residents and attending and get that protection.

3) **LIFE INSURANCE PROTECTION**: Once you've crunched the numbers, you find you have a little left over, you might also be able to get life insurance protection. Again, you should work with an agent who knows what he or she is doing (years of experience, types of clients, etc). In most cases, the agent you are working with for long-term disability protection should be able to help you with a life insurance policy, too. So, make sure to ask them what your options are.

Remember, though, that while life insurance is great for the people you leave behind, at this stage, it's more important to have long-term disability protection so if you need both you may have to strike a balance between the two types of coverage. This is where it is really helpful to work with an experienced agent.

SECTION III

CASH FLOW MANAGEMENT

SECTION III: CASH FLOW MANAGEMENT

The car pile-up had changed Mary's life in more ways than one. Not only had she become more conscious of her own mortality, but she'd realized precisely how bad her financial situation was. She'd finally admitted to herself that she was in trouble and she had to take control of her finances. She could no longer afford to channel every ostrich in existence and stick her head in the sand every time financial issues came up.

She'd taken Jennifer's advice on the importance of protection to heart, but when she went to get more information on policies and the related costs, she realized she'd be hard pressed to make the monthly premiums. But she had no choice. She'd have to find a way because the risk was too great.

So, Mary decided it was time to approach Jennifer again and ask her for some advice. Her roommate was more than happy to help.

"I did as you told me and checked out a few policies, but I can't really see how I'm going to pay the premiums. I'm barely managing as it is," Mary said with a pout.

Jennifer cocked an eyebrow. "You know we both make about the same amount of money, don't you?"

"Yeah, I do. It's why I was convinced your parents help you. You never seem to run out of money and you definitely live better than I do. It just reinforces how unimpressive my financial skills are. How do you do it?"

"First off, you're in the same boat as many of our colleagues and it has nothing to do with talent and everything to do with education. If no one taught you how to manage your finances properly, you can't expect to be able to do it blindly.

Secondly, it's all about cash flow management. Learning to manage your cash flow effectively is the key to financial success and freedom, no matter how much money you make."

"Cash flow management? I'm having a bit of a blonde moment because I have no clue what that is." Mary had discovered that Jennifer was a great teacher, even though she wasn't technically the expert. Her roommate refused to take credit because she claimed she was just repeating what her family's financial advisor had taught her. But Mary was still adamant it had a lot to do with Jennifer because she never felt like a fool and was comfortable asking any question. And her roommate was always patient and had a knack for simplifying complex concepts.

"Cash flow is simply the money coming in and going out. So, it's the money you earn and the money you spend, i.e. the cash that flows into your account and the cash that flows out of your account. And managing your income and expenses effectively is the difference between failure and success on a financial level.

Let me explain it like my parent's financial advisor explained it to me. The example he gave really stuck with me because I was shocked." At Mary's curious look, Jennifer continued, "You'll see why in just a moment."

"Let's consider the athletes that play in the NFL. Out of the 1.1 million kids out there that play high school football, only 0.15% go on to play in the professionals. Think about that! Less than 1,700 players are in the league (32 teams and 53 players per team), which means that less than 1,700 high school players out of 1,100,000 will ever participate at that level."

"Wow! Okay, that's pretty tough," Mary said.

Jennifer nodded. "What's funny is that my brother and my dad will yell at the TV, screaming that these guys 'suck' when something they didn't like happened. I'm not into the whole football thing but I still ask them both how well they could do on that field. Shuts them up pretty quick. And there's a lot of grumbling about how women don't understand sports," she said, rolling her eyes.

Mary chuckled. "My dad's the same."

"Boys will be boys. Anyway, moving on. So, like in any industry, the people that are the best will typically get paid the most. The average NFL playing career is 3.5 years and the average cumulative earnings during that career is $6.7m[iv] (2013 USA TODAY Article)."

Mary's eyes widened. "That's a lot of money in a short time! No wonder everyone wants to become a football player. I would too. I mean they earn enough money in 3.5 years to live almost the rest of their lives without having to work ever again."

"See, that's not the whole story. Sadly, there is another statistic that goes along with these high-profile professionals. Five years after their playing careers are over, roughly 78% of these athletes are completely broke[v]. Think about that for a moment. Graduate college at 22-years old and go pro. Retire from the league five-years later at age 27. Declare bankruptcy at age 32. Seems completely crazy that could happen, but unfortunately it is a probable outcome for the typical NFL athlete."

"Are you sure they go broke? You aren't pulling my leg, are you?"

"Yes, I'm sure. You hear special interest stories in the news about how these athletes go broke. These stories sell magazines and advertising because for some weird reason, people like hearing about celebrities being miserable."

"How can they be broke? Seriously? I mean, I know I suck at managing my finances but with all that money, couldn't they hire a financial advisor or something? I mean, they could at least save a big chunk of their earnings. An entire family can live off $100,000 a year and yet they can't save anything even when they're making an obscene amount of money?" Mary didn't know why but she was suddenly feeling a little more superior. Yeah, she was struggling financially but she was earning a pittance by comparison. If she'd been earning that kind of money, she would have never ended up in the same situation.

"Okay, let's try a little exercise. Imagine for a moment that you find yourself sitting in a crowded coffee shop. There is only one open chair and it's at the small table where you happen to be seated. A very large young man asks to sit with you. You end up making small talk and you find out that a reputable NFL team recently drafted him. He isn't going to be a marquee player, but he is still well on his way to earning $5,000,000 over the next five-years. He shares with you that he's heard the stories about all the players that go broke and he is concerned.

Help him out. What are you going to tell him?"

Mary stopped to think for a moment. "Well, I guess I'd tell him to stop spending on silly things and save most of his money."

"Anything else?"

"I guess I'd also tell him to avoid making the same stupid financial mistakes I did and to get educated on how to manage his money properly."

"Okay, that's definitely good. And what about his future? The longer he can play, the more money he can make, right?"

Mary nodded enthusiastically. "I'd definitely tell him to invest in himself to be healthy and stay fit so maybe he can last longer than 27, which means he'll have even more money to save."

"So, to recap, you'd tell him to:

1. Save a large percentage of his annual income;

2. Keep his costs as low as possible;

3. Avoid financial mistakes;

4. Invest in his greatest asset, namely longevity in his career."

"Exactly," Mary said with a grin. She was feeling pretty proud of herself.

"That's all great advice. I'm guessing you're feeling really good about yourself. I mean, clearly your financial intellect is better developed than most NFL players, right?"

Mary hesitated. "I guess so," she said, but she wasn't all that convinced. Jennifer's tone made her much less certain than she'd been a minute ago.

"Okay, then answer me this. If it is so easy and you know what to do, what are you doing with your money? Are you following the advice that you just delivered to that young NFL rookie?"

"You can't compare me with an NFL player. I'm earning peanuts by comparison!" Mary exclaimed.

"Actually, it's a valid comparison. The same principles apply, no matter how much money you earn.

And if you think things will get better when you graduate to attending, you might be surprised that it isn't. Hidden in plain view is a financial truth when comparing the career earnings of the average NFL player to the career earnings of a specialty specific medical doctor. Using the Human Life Value calculation, an orthopedic surgeon that is five-years into her career as an attending might earn in the neighborhood of $335,000 per year. When you multiply that against the Human Life Value multiplier for a present value number, you get $6.7m. And keep in mind that $6.7m career earnings of an NFL player is an average. Some make more, and some make less. In that view, specialty specific medical doctors roughly earn the same amount over their careers as an NFL player. The only difference is that the medical doctor is earning those dollars over a longer period."

"So, what are you saying exactly?" asked Mary, feeling slightly giddy at the amount of money she could potentially make over the course of her career.

"I'm saying that you have the same potential to end up broke at the end of your career as that NFL player.

Imagine for a moment that you are 65-years old today and you are about to retire. Consider the amount of money that you would need to have sitting in a lump sump to recreate your $335,000 annual income. Based on the Trinity Study[vi], one can withdraw 4% from a well-diversified portfolio over an extended period of time and not run out of money. To get $335,000 per year at 4% per annum, you will need $8,375,000 using the following formula:

Desired Annual Income / 4% Withdrawal Rate = Required Lump Sum

Think about every medical doctor you know in the hospital that is near retirement. How many of them do you think have a net worth close to $10,000,000? Most of them? Half? Less than half?"

"Less than half, I guess. It's not like any of them leave their financials lying around or post their net worth online or anything."

"It's probably a lot less than half. Of course, the percentages may not all be the same in terms of returns. And some people may not desire to replicate the same standard of living in retirement as they do during their working years. That said, there are a large percentage of Americans that are nowhere near ready for retirement. We don't hear about it like we hear about the NFL players because nobody cares to watch an ESPN 30 for 30 about the orthopedic surgeon that went broke."

"I'd watch a show like that. At least to learn what mistakes I should avoid making," Mary said.

"I would too, but I doubt any network will make a show for an audience of two people," Jennifer replied with a chuckle.

"Okay, so, basically, what you're saying is that if learn to manage my cash flow properly, not only do I have a good chance of not going broke but I might even to get to that $10 million net worth, right?"

"Right. I'm surprised, though, that you aren't telling me that you're too young to worry about retirement…"

"Honestly, part of me is saying exactly that but then there's this other part of me that wants to think and plan ahead. I guess you're rubbing off on me," Mary grinned.

"That's definitely good. So, back to our cash flow management lesson. If there's one single thing you remember from our talks, it has to be:

> # THE GREATEST DETERMINANT BETWEEN FINANCIAL SUCCESS AND FINANCIAL FAILURE IS PROPER CASH FLOW MANAGEMENT

"Cash Flow Management is the greatest determinant between a life of financial success or a life of financial failure. This is very clear in the world of business. If your business expenses are greater than your revenues, you won't have enough money to deliver value to the marketplace through a product or service and, eventually, you will go out of business. For individuals and families, the timing of the cash flow extends beyond the timeline required for the business.

For businesses, revenues are required while the business is in operation. Once the business is taken out of operation, you don't have the expenses anymore and as such you do not need the revenues either.

Human beings are different. Humans approaching retirement age desire to cease operations that generate revenue, but they continue to have operational expenses in terms of food, shelter, medical costs, etc. for an indeterminate amount of time. For some, retirement lasts a short time, while for others retirement may last 40 years or more."

Mary blinked. She suddenly felt really overwhelmed. Now Jennifer was talking about businesses. "Huh?"

Jennifer smiled. "Okay, so think of it like this. The café we go to all the time needs to have money coming in while it's open so it can keep buying all the stuff it needs to make the coffee they sell. Now, if they were to close down, they wouldn't need to make money anymore, right? There wouldn't be any expenses, so the business wouldn't need an income."

"I get it now. For us, retirement is like closing the store. We no longer have an income but we will still have expenses even after 'closing', and those expenses can last for quite a while so we need a way to cover them."

"Exactly," Jennifer replied, smiling in pride. For some reason, that really made Mary feel good about herself. She was actually starting to get this stuff, and it wasn't as hard as she had feared. Most of it was actually common sense, but without someone to point it out to her, she'd never have realized all the implications.

"Okay, now teach me how to manage my cash flow properly," Mary said, practically bouncing with excitement. Had anyone told her a week ago that she'd be excited about learning how to manage her money properly, she would have told them they were insane and needed to see a specialist immediately. How quickly things changed.

THE 30-SECOND BUDGET

"Effective cash flow management is all about making sure you aren't spending more than you are making, in the simplest form. The first step is to put together a very simple budget. Don't give me that horrified look. I said simple and I meant very simple so relax."

"Okay, I'm listening."

"As I said, we're going to avoid going crazy with your budget. Budgets can get complex and messy really fast. Detailed household budgets do not typically work all that well because they are hard to follow. They are easy to set-up and agree to, but sticking to them is difficult. In many respects, they are the financial equivalent of a diet. We all know how simple diets and losing weight can be, on a theoretical level. Just track all of your eating, keep your food intake low, and exercise. Simple! It is so simple that we live in a nation where obesity is epidemic. So, no, I'm not going to force you to put together an itemized budget."

"Thank goodness for that," Mary replied in relief.

"Of course, if you like that kind of thing, we could do a line-by-line budget with expense categories and everything," Jennifer offered slyly.

Mary cocked an eyebrow. "No way. No thanks. I'm cool with simple. But why do I suddenly think your budget is so detailed it would make an accountant proud?"

Jennifer blushed. "Maybe," she muttered. "But I'm not going to show you mine because I don't want to overwhelm you. Instead, we're going to consider the 30-second budget, which is how I started out. So, what you do is this:

- FIRST, flow 20% of your income towards Long Term Wealth Building.

- SECOND, flow 30% towards taxes. You have to pay them.

- THIRD, flow 50% towards your lifestyle.

That's it. You don't need a row of jelly jars that all have the name of some household expense that you are required to put money in every payday. No envelopes. No complicated computer programs or phone apps."

"I know you said simple but that sounds almost too simple. But you say it works, so I'm not going to question it," Mary said resolutely.

"Good choice," Jennifer said with a wink.

"So, basically, with my $55,000 in wages, I should put $11,000 towards long-term wealth building, $16,500 towards taxes and the remaining $27,500 goes towards my lifestyle."

"Yes and no. The long-term wealth building section of the budget isn't something you should be worrying about right now. Not only will blocking out $11,000 a year from your wages make life harder right now, once you become an attending, you can save that much in a little over two months. The returns aren't substantial enough to warrant you struggling right now."

"Okay, that's good. But what about my loans? Shouldn't they be under a separate section?"

"No, they fall under lifestyle expenses. But we'll get into managing your debt in just a moment," Jennifer assured her.

~~~~~~~~~~~

WHY I UTILIZE THE 30-SECOND BUDGET

Mary's initial reaction of complete and utter horror at the mention of the word budget is very common. I discovered early on in my career how much most people hate budgeting. Even if they enjoy putting the spreadsheet together – yes, there are people who like creating spreadsheets – and are happy to spend hours putting together the perfect budget. When it comes time to implement and stick to their perfect budget, then the whole thing goes out the window. This is often because they've gone overboard with their itemization. It is impossible to predict to with accuracy exactly what your expenses will be in the next month. People will try to come up with a fantastic budget and then in the second week they'll get hit with an unexpected expense. Or, they'll temporarily revert back to old spending habits and by the time they get to the end of the month they feel defeated and give up.

The 30-second budget is set up to be simple. Three main categories – stay within the rails. If you mess-up, you can adjust across all of your spending inside the 50% lifestyle category. Just split your money up into three according to the aforementioned percentages and redirect it as necessary. Many of my clients actually set up a system whereby they redirect their money towards their long-term wealth building plans and taxes automatically so there is no temptation.

When setting up your initial budget, though, please consider your initial income and your life as it is right now. Then, rework the budget for what you think it might look like five-years from now. Most of the residency programs where I've spoken over the years are filled with dedicated physicians who have put their lives on hold so they can focus on their education and training. Once residency ends, many of these professionals go on to get married and some even have children.

When children arrive in a relationship, sometimes one or both parents decide they might want to pull back from work to spend more time with their child. If you think this might be you, you should design your budget around that income scenario instead of dual income with no kids. Give specific attention to your housing decisions and your automobile decisions. A dual-income, no-kids scenario will be able to purchase a lot of house. If you build your long-term budget around that income scenario and then, three-years later, one of the incomes goes to zero, that family can find themselves feeling just as broke as they were during residency. Or worse.

~~~~~~~~~~~

DEBT AND CASH FLOW MANAGEMENT

"So, now let's talk about debt. I want you to think back to the day when you signed the paperwork to borrow the bulk of the money to attend medical school. How hard was that? Did the bank seem overly reluctant or did they seem pretty happy to sign you up?" Jennifer asked.

"To be honest, it was the easiest thing I've ever done. I was worried because my parents warned me that it could be difficult to get all that money – they've never had much luck getting loans because of their low incomes. But with me, they practically rolled out the red carpet," Mary explained.

Jennifer nodded. "That's the case with most med school students. The reason is that banks see you as a good risk to take. You are a future high-income earner and you are willing to work really hard to achieve a long-term goal."

"I'm a good risk? Not sure I understand what you mean."

"Banks don't lend you money out of the goodness of their hearts. They're not charities. They want to make money, which is where the interest they charge on the loan comes in. Now, lending money is a risky business. And banks don't like risk. They want to make sure they recover their money and their profit. So, they look at everything, from your job history to the properties you own and the financial decisions you've made throughout your life to decide whether they will lend you money or not.

The less risk you pose – i.e. being a good risk – the happier they are to give you money. And, as a future attending physician with the potential to lend a heck of a lot of money, the banks is more than sure they'll recover the money they lend you.

Some banks extend this philosophy to their mortgage departments and offer special financing arrangements to physicians to purchase homes, because they want to take advantage of the low risk you pose as much as possible. You're pretty much the goose that laid the golden egg for a bank."

Mary mulled Jennifer's words over. It made sense. Funnily enough, she'd never really given much thought to how banks worked. "I've considered banks nothing but a necessary evil since I can remember. Especially after all the ranting from my parents about how banks are evil incarnate and are trying to bury the regular person, not allowing them to get ahead. I never stopped to really think about why. I get it now, though."

"In a way, they really are nothing more than a necessary evil. But that's a discussion for another time. The important thing you need to remember is that, as a future attending physician, when it comes to banks, you have the power because they want your business. In fact, they are desperate for it because they have few clients who are in such a good place as you will be. That's why they're so happy to give you money as a med student. They're hoping to build a relationship with you so that 10 years down the line, when you're earning a massive paycheck, you'll continue to borrow money from them rather than another bank.

Just a quick side note, before we get into the discussion about eliminating student debt. When it comes to housing, you should consider capping your household mortgage cash flow at 15%. If you decide you want to exceed that, look across your budget to find the funds for the extra percentages. For example, if you really care about your house but don't really care about cars, then move some of the monthly car cash flow towards housing. Also, remember that this 15% is inside the 50% of your annual lifestyle cash flow that we discussed earlier.

I know this probably isn't a concern right now, but it's a good tip to remember for the future. Now, let's talk about getting rid of those pesky student loans."

ELIMINATING STUDENT LOAN DEBT

"Now, if you're anything like me, you're probably wondering right now what the best way to pay off your student loans is. It's something all residents ponder, at one point or another. The thing is that there isn't one simple answer to this question and it isn't always clear cut or something you can easily plug into a spreadsheet calculator for the answer. The reason lies in the number of potential variables and some of those variables are subjective.

For example, someone who is completely debt adverse to the point where they literally lose sleep each night because of their student loans, then it's probably a good idea for that person to be more aggressive in settling their loans over other cash flow priorities in their life. In this case, the student loan is infringing on their sense of financial balance so much that the lack of sleep will start affecting other areas of their life. Even if they have a large block of debt at a low interest rate and a long amortization, it just makes sense to prioritize the payoff of the student loans in this case because of the subjective psychological factors at play.

Conversely, someone else may have the same fact pattern, but they don't care about the debt. It doesn't cause them any angst whatsoever. In this case, a block of debt that is financed at historically low interest rates is a tool they can use. In this case, it makes more sense for this person to pay the minimum payment and allow the loan to run its course."

Mary cocked her head. "So, let's see if I'm getting better with this finance thing. What you're saying is that if my student loans are driving me nuts and I'm so freaked out about them that I can't sleep at night, and this stress has started affecting the rest of my life, then I really should be doing everything I can to pay off my loans as quickly as possible, no matter how attractive the loan is."

"Exactly!" Jennifer replied excitedly, glad to see her 'student' was progressing. "And if you don't mind the loans, you can use the money you'd otherwise use to pay off the loans for other things you might finance at a higher interest rate (like a car), but only those things that would benefit you financially over the long term. We don't want to waste money pointlessly. Paying off debt isn't ALWAYS about economics only, sometimes it is also about psychology. If that low interest debt is causing you stress, then it might make sense to pay it off."

"Okay, that makes sense. So, let's say I want to try to pay off my loans as quickly as possible. Is there any way I can do it without living on beans on toast?"

"There is a strategy you can use to pay off all your loans earlier without adding any additional out of pocket cash flow. However, it will require a loan portfolio consisting of a number of different loans. A number of the loans must be financed over a shorter period and then one or two or the larger loans can be at the usual 20-year financing duration.

The strategy is simple. When you are in a position to start paying the fully amortized payments across all of your loans, stay consistent in paying that amount until the first loan is completely paid off.

Let's say that first loan had a monthly payment of $100. Once that first loan is completely paid off, then direct that $100 towards the next smallest loan amount. This will accelerate your ability to pay off that second loan because you are now putting an extra $100 each month towards the principal of the loan. Once the second loan is fully paid off, you then do the same thing and keep applying the same gross amount of payment across the remaining loans.

Depending on your loan structure, you could potentially reduce the total time it takes you to pay off your loans by 25% or more."

"Another approach, which would only require a little extra outlay on your part, would involve paying a little extra every month on one of your loans. Let's say you have four loans, one for $25,000 over 7 years, one for $50,000 over 10 years, another for $75,000 over 20 years and the last one for $80,000, also over 20 years. All these loans are at a 7 percent interest rate. Your full payment every month on each loan would be $377, $580, $581 and $620, respectively.

Now, if you were to pay an extra $25 every month on your first loan, you could have your first loan paid off in 6 years and 5 months. Once you closed out that loan, you'd take the $377 payment plus the extra $25 and put it towards the second loan. With the additional payment, you could close out that loan in 8.5 years, after which, you'd put the initial $377, plus $25, and the payment towards the second loan of $580 towards the third loan. With the extra payments, you'd be able to close the loan out in a total of 12 years, at which point, you'd put all those extra payments towards the last loan of $80,000, which you'd end up closing out at the 14-year mark.

So, with a mere $25 extra every month, you could close out all your loans in 14 years and, while you're at it, you'll also save over $31,000 in interest."

Mary's eyes widened. "Wow, that's really impressive. It would probably be even more impressive if I could start the ball rolling with an extra $100 per month, right?"

"Definitely. Now, there's no need to get ahead of yourself or to beat yourself up if you can't always make the extra payment. That's why I think it's always best to commit to a smaller figure, like $25 every month, which is a couple of fancy cups of coffee, than a larger amount. You know you can always scrounge up $25 to make the additional payment, but $100 might be more difficult some months. Commit to $25 and then pay more when you can."

"Definitely good advice. And I live that I won't be killing my cash flow to get rid of these loans as fast as possible."

"Exactly. That's why we have the 30-Second Budget, where the cash flows being applied to student loans live in the 50% that goes towards lifestyle expense. Provided you've stayed true to the 30-Second Budget, once the loans are all paid off, you can direct ALL of that monthly money towards improving your lifestyle."

"There's one important warning I need to give you, though. Beware of consolidation loan companies that market to you and offer you lower monthly payments. They may not be a better deal for you and can actually result in higher costs and a longer loan duration. For example, a 10-year loan of $25,000 financed at 6% has a monthly payment of $278/month. An offer may come in to reduce your monthly payment on that loan by 30% to $194/month. Sounds pretty good! Then you look at the fine print. The new loan is for 20-years at 7% interest. A quick comparison of the two loans can be achieved by multiplying the number of years by 12 and then by the amount of the payment.

<u>Original Loan:</u>

10 years x 12 months in a year x 278 = $33,360

<u>Proposed Loan:</u>

20 years x 12 months in a year x 194 = $46,560

This comparison shows that by 'saving' 30% on your monthly payment, you'll actually end-up spending $13,200 more over the course of the loan.

Before you refinance any debt, make sure you completely understand all the terms and compare all costs until the loan is fully paid-off."

"Okay, so, don't jump on the bandwagon until I've crunched the numbers. Got it," Mary said with a pleased grin.

CASH FLOW IS MOST IMPORTANT

Mary discovered that Cash Flow Management is the single greatest determinant of financial success or financial failure. One of the most common reasons why businesses, NFL players and medical doctors go broke during their lifetimes is that they spend the majority of their Lifetime Cash Flow in the present and give little consideration to the cash flow they will need in retirement.

If you are still in residency, the year that you make the jump from resident to attending represents the greatest cash flow opportunity you'll ever experience in your lifetime. In one year, your income will jump by multiples. You have the opportunity to give yourself a substantial lifestyle increase while building a strong savings plan at the same time. The savings plan can be built in such that it will not impact your lifestyle at all provided you structure your cash flow properly during this one-year and stick to the plan.

SECTION III: ACTION ITEMS

1) **5-YEARS POST RESIDENCY** - Imagine what you want your life to look like five-years into your career as an attending. Where are you living? Who are you living with? What life changes do you expect will occur during that time? Will you have children? Will you and your partner both continue to work at the same pace and earnings or is it desirable that one or both of you might pull back from work? Consider these questions carefully and decide if it would be prudent to build slack into your budget. The decisions that you make here will have the largest impact on how you choose to spend towards housing (15% of monthly cash flow max) and cars.

2) **30-SECOND BUDGET** - Build your budget around your expected first-year attending salary while taking into account the things you wrote down in the previous exercise. If you came to the conclusion that you want to build in 10% slack into your budget, then simply add that amount to your savings category such that for the first 5-years you are saving 30%, taxes 30% and lifestyle is 40%. Then, when the lifestyle change occurs, you can simply shift to saving 20%, taxes 30% and lifestyle 50%. Email me at john.crane@ffgadvisors.com. for a cash flow spreadsheet that you can use to build, test and measure different cash flow scenarios for yourself.

---

3) **<u>STUDENT LOAN MANAGEMENT</u>** - Review your student loans. If they don't make sense to you, call the loan servicing company and ask them to explain them to you. Ask your existing servicing company if they have the ability to reduce your interest rate. Sometimes they will have special programs where they can consolidate your more expensive loans and give you better loan terms. Beware of companies that market to you with loan consolidation programs. Their attractive sounding offer might not be a better deal for you - even if they are offering a lower monthly payment.

SECTION IV

THERE IS NO FREE LUNCH

SECTION IV: THERE IS NO FREE LUNCH

Mary couldn't believe it. It was finally time. She was a few days from finishing her residency and officially becoming an attending. She knew she'd still have a lot to deal with, but she already had a few offers from different hospitals and she was pleased. She'd picked her top one and already had a meeting with a Contracts Attorney that she hired to review the contract before she signed. If there was one thing Jennifer had taught her, it was to always consult an expert.

She was incredibly grateful to her roommate. Without her, she would have been in a much deeper financial hole than she was now. Nothing drove that point home more than the sprained ankle she'd gotten by being silly and not looking where she was going. She had to stay offer her feet for a little while, but it was nothing serious. However, it drove the point home how the unexpected can happen – especially when you least expect it. She was glad, at that point, that she had good long-term disability protection, even if she hadn't needed it. It was just nice knowing she had that safety net available.

Now, she knew there was one last area to tackle, namely to get to that $10 million net worth so she could have a comfortable retirement. But she wasn't worried anymore because she'd made the best decision she'd ever made, after becoming a doctor, of course, and that was to hire a financial advisor. In fact, she was on her way at that moment to discuss her financial situation and how she could make the most out of it. Life was definitely good and so much less stressful knowing a professional had her back.

BUILDING WEALTH

Mary learned a lot of important lessons from Jennifer that brought her financial balance, and gave her a stepping stone to start her new life on the right foot. And now, she's gotten to the point where she realizes she has to look to the far future, which is where wealth-building comes in.

~~~~~~~~~~~~

When I joined my firm in 2002, they trained me on how to help clients manage their investments. The philosophy that they taught me is called Active Management. Active Management is based on three main tenants:

1) Pick the right stocks and trade them in advance of market movements such that you make money consistently and reliably.

2) Correctly time markets and trade them in advance of market movements such that you make money consistently and reliably.

3) Possess the ability to correctly choose the Professional Money Managers that can pick the

right stocks and time markets such that they make money for their investors consistently and reliably.

The Active Managers that I was using expressed their philosophy in terms of keeping portfolio volatility lower than the general markets will help clients lose less in down markets such that when markets recovered the portfolios would outperform when markets recovered.

From 2002 to 2007, the stock market kept going up so, to my clients, I looked really smart. That was until the markets went down sharply in 2008/2009 due to the mortgage crisis. The markets tanked and so did the portfolios that I had invested my clients' money in. The smoother is better philosophy did not play out exactly as described by the fund companies. My clients didn't perform worse than the markets, but they didn't perform much better either. From my vantage point, the higher fees that clients paid to be in these strategies just wasn't worth it.

Wanting to get to the bottom of it, I approached the fund companies and asked to meet with their regional representatives. They came in for a meeting with me.

"When we first met, you explained your investment philosophy to me and the mantra was smoother is better." I opened with this to refresh their memories.

"Yes, that is our mantra!"

"But, it didn't happen that way," I retorted.

"John, what happened in 2008-2009 was unprecedented. Unprecedented! You see, there were these mortgages. The mortgages were bundled into securities and sold on the exchanges. When people didn't pay their mortgages, the bonds went bad and the market collapsed. It was UNPRECEDENTED!"

That was a nice recap, but it really didn't explain why the whole smoother-is-better thing didn't work out. What got said next really got my attention.

"The good news is that we've created a whole new platform. It's called Tactical Asset Reallocation. You see, the next time something like 2008-2009 is about to happen, our Money Managers will shift your client assets to something safe. Then, when the bad thing has passed, we'll move the client assets back into the market," the fund company representative said with enthusiasm. By now, my head was about on its side as I looked at him. I couldn't believe what I was hearing.

"Wow. Assuming that I believe you can actually do that, my question to you right now is this: Where were you guys 30 months ago? If you can predict severe market drops, I would have expected to get a phone call from you all."

After a prolonged pregnant pause, the fund representative went right back into his prepared remarks about how the market drop of 2008-2009 was unprecedented. UNPRECEDENTED!!

For me, the meeting was over and now I had a problem. The investment philosophy that I had been following did not prove to be reliable during one of the worst market drops in modern times. If there was ever a case study, that market window was it and the soundness of their algorithm didn't prove out.

Over the next 12 months, I interviewed advisors that had a lot of money under management to find out what they were doing. The responses were split. Some were using the same fund platforms that I had been using and through gritted teeth had accepted the unprecedented argument. Others told me about an investment approach called Structured Investing that took a more passive approach to asset management. This fund company happened to be holding an Adviser Conference in New York City in the coming weeks. I paid my money and traveled up to New York to learn more.

This fund company is unique in that across their Board of Directors are people from academia. Professors from some of the top educational institutions in America. Nobel Prize winners in their respective areas of Finance and Economics. Some of these leaders from the world of academia were at the conference and taught some of the sessions. One of these professors led his session with this question for the audience of 600 investment advisors:

"If it were possible to pick the right stocks and make money consistently and reliably, or if it were possible to time markets and make money consistently and reliably, then WHY? WHY WOULD WALL STREET NEED YOUR CLIENTS MONEY?!?", the professor asked the audience. Most of the audience were long time investors with this company, so they already knew the punch line. I sat there in a stunned silence for a moment as the question washed over me.

Selfishly, if I could pick the right stocks and trade markets consistently and reliably, I'd want to maximize my profits. If it were a no-lose deal, I would only need a little seed money to get started and then I would just sit there and grow my base of assets to billions. Trillions even! The answer to the question is that Wall Street **would not** need my clients' money or anyone's money for that matter. They certainly wouldn't dilute their profits by sharing their winnings with a bunch of strangers.

What I learned from the market drop of 2008-2009 was that markets move in the short term for lots of reasons and some of those reasons have nothing to do with finance. They have to do with the emotions of fear and greed. Over the long term, the value of the markets move due to the underlying value of the assets that make up the markets. Companies. Companies that build a thing or provide a service for a profit. The markets are made up of 12,000+ companies that are all working towards the goal of serving their customers and turning a profit for their owners. The owners are the shareholders. If you own a single stock based mutual fund, then you are a part owner of the businesses that make up the mutual fund that you hold. Over the long term, it is the value of the 12,000+ individual companies that drive returns. Not the money managers.

There is no free lunch. It is not a secret that specialty specific medical doctors are high-income earners. This makes you an attractive target for client acquisition for many different industries. It also makes you an attractive target for high-risk investments and scams. At some point, it is highly likely that you'll be approached for an investment in a start-up company, a strip mall or even a car wash. It might be a good deal. It might not. If you just can't tell, the best approach is typically to stay on the sidelines. If you think you might want to invest, assemble a team of professionals (attorney, accountant, corporate financial analyst) that can help you evaluate the opportunity from your position and your interests. Absent an advisory team that represents your interests, a good place to start is with the same question that was asked of the room full of 600 investment advisors in

NYC that day: If it's possible to make so much money, then why? Why are you coming to me with this opportunity?

SECTION IV: ACTION ITEMS

1) <u>CHOOSE AN INVESTMENT PHILOSOPHY</u> -

The stock market most commonly plays a role in most Americans' long-term wealth building in the form of employer-provided retirement accounts. Decide upon an overall investment philosophy and then stick to that philosophy over the long term. For recommended reading on the topic, you may want to look at **A Random Walk Down Wall Street by Burton Makiel**.

2) <u>BEHAVIOR MATTERS</u> - The company

DALBAR monitors and tracks actual investor returns. DALBAR's report entitled Annual Quantitative Analysis of Investor Behavior is one of the most commonly referenced documents by investment management companies. In this study, DALBAR compares one of the major stock market indices (the S&P 500) with actual investor returns over a sliding 20-year period. The comparison shows that the unmanaged S&P 500 typically outperforms the average investor during these 20-year periods between 3-5%! The reason for the performance gap is Investor Behavior is typically poor. The average investor will buy and sell their investments at the wrong times. Hold equities for the long term, diversify, rebalance and BEHAVE!

3) __BE SKEPTICAL AND ASK THE QUESTION__ -

If this investment opportunity is such a lock for me, then why do you need my money to make it work? Why aren't you mortgaging your house and borrowing money from everyone you know instead of talking to me? When it comes to investing, learn to ask a lot of questions and/or surround yourself with an advisory team that represents your interests and can help you ask those questions.

SECTION V

SUMMARY

SECTION V: SUMMARY

Every resident and/or resident fellow reading this book has the capacity to enjoy a great career and a great life. Depending on where you are in your training, you may be on the precipice of achieving a substantial life goal of becoming an Attending Physician and I wish to congratulate you on that tremendous accomplishment. Not just for you, but for the public and patients that you've worked so hard to serve.

Protection Matters. Know what your Human Life Value is and the impact it would have on your financial plan if your paycheck were to permanently disappear.

Cash Flow Management is Most Important. As you transition from resident to attending, you have the great opportunity to structure your cash flows with a 20% savings rate while simultaneously experiencing a 2x or 3x increase in your lifestyle (based on a $50,000 resident salary and a $200,000 attending income). By building in the savings in the year you make the jump to attending, you will never miss the money. You will never have gotten the opportunity to become addicted to it. Remember our NFL player? What great advice did you have for him? Remember that advice because if it was good for him, it's probably good for you to follow as well.

No free lunch. If you do not remember anything from that chapter, please remember this: "If it were possible to make easy money, then why? Why do you need my money?"

One of my favorite quotes is "Education without implementation is merely entertainment." Please do not allow this book to become merely entertainment. Let it motivate you to take control of your financial management and set-up a lifelong financial plan that will provide well for you and your loved ones. If the topic bores you, then let this book motivate you to hire a qualified adviser to help you implement these things for you.

Take action today.

THANK YOU FOR READING MY BOOK!

~~~~~~~~~~

Your time is valuable and I appreciate the time you took to read my book. Now here comes the most important part…

Implementation.

The ideas and the knowledge contained in this book **will only benefit you _if_ you take action**. If you are unsure or you lack the time, please take this book to your advisor or give my offices a call.

Please let me know how we can help.
http://www.cranefinancial.com/contact

FREQUENTLY ASKED QUESTIONS

FREQUENTLY ASKED QUESTIONS

I'm still early in my residency training, what financial moves should I be making right now?

Cash flow allocation at this stage of your career is a balance because of the relatively low salaries that are paid to PGY medical professionals. This allocation won't work for everyone, but the priorities I believe are consistent across most medical doctors.

1) Protection - Please re-read the section on Protection Matters. Through the medical training you've done and that you are a few years away from completing, you will have built a multimillion-dollar asset within yourself. The way you will convert that multimillion-dollar asset into cash that you can use and enjoy will be through your physical ability to deliver what you've learned to patients by serving them. If you lose your ability to serve patients (you cannot choose your disability, so think brain injury or a stroke), then the multimillion-dollar asset you've built can no longer be converted into cash that you can use. Purchase the best and the most long-term disability insurance that you can afford as early as you can. Some insurance companies will allow you to purchase a contract using age based pricing, so the premium for a fairly robust contract will be in the $100-$200/month range while you are still in residency. Long-term

disability insurance isn't fun, but think of all the people you've met over the years in the emergency room. Every single one of them woke up that day with other plans. Nobody thinks they will end-up disabled. However, according to the Personal Disability Quotient Calculator provided by the Council for Disability Awareness, the typical male, aged 29, at 5'10", weighing 170lbs, who leads a healthy lifestyle and has a somewhat more active indoor job than an office job, has a 22% chance of becoming disabled for 3 months or more. If they do become disabled, they stand a 32% chance of that disability lasting 5 years or longer. The same calculator shows that woman, aged 29, at 5'4", weighing 125lbs, leading the same life as her male counterpart has a 26% chance of becoming disabled for three months or more, and if they do become disabled for 3 months, they have a 32% chance of that disability last 5 years or longer. Those aren't statistics you can afford to ignore.

2) Cash Savings - Holding a modest cash reserve account will help you when you have unplanned expenses and avoid the need to use credit to help you fund your lifestyle.

~~~~~~~~~

We have insurance salespeople in here all the time that tell me that I should by long-term disability

insurance right now because it will be cheaper for me to buy it now. Is that true?

Yes. 1) You are as young and as healthy as you will ever be over your lifetime. Insurance premiums are calculated based on health and age. 2) Some insurance companies will sign agreements with hospitals to offer the contracts at a small discount to residents provided the residents purchase the contract while still in residency. Just make sure the discounted contract language is consistent with what you'd expect from a top tier long-term disability contract from a reputable insurance company.

The more pressing reason why you should buy it today is to protect your future income. Over my career, I've seen a couple of examples where a resident doctor chose to wait and then developed a health issue that made getting the contract impossible. For those doctors, the disability insurance they wanted, but waited to purchase is off limits. This impacts their career decisions. For example: the doctor that waited and can no longer purchase coverage can't join a practice that doesn't offer a group long term disability plan. This doctor has to be concerned about pre-existing conditions language that might be in the group LTD plan. This doctor must take insurance into account when choosing jobs where if they had bought the contract early would have more career flexibility.

~~~~~~~~~

Should I hire a contracts lawyer to review my job offers before I sign-on for my first attending job?

Absolutely, unequivocally **YES!** One of my colleagues in this space tells a great story about a work contract that he reviewed with a clause stating that the physician agrees to live in the medical office compound! The owner of the practice had purchased a condo close to the medical office and was requiring in the employment contract that his new employee to rent and live in that condo. That is an extreme example, but to the uninformed who is just anxious to start working as a full attending the contract vetting by a professional that is solely representing them can potentially be worth more than the attorney fee.

As a new attending, you aren't going to have great bargaining and negotiating power, but a skilled attorney in this area can provide you with two main benefits:

1) Understanding your contract - The attorney will break your contract down and explain it to you in plain English. Know what you are agreeing to and the pros/cons of each from your perspective. Do not rely on the employers' lawyer.

2) Understanding what might be negotiable and coaching you on the negotiations.

The cost of a contract review might cost you a few thousand dollars, but the cost of signing a bad contract could end up costing you tens of thousands or more.

~~~~~~~~~~

A financial advisor told me that I need to buy a wealth building life insurance policy because it provides me with tax-deferred growth. Is that a good idea?

Long term that might be a good idea, but every person is different and every set of circumstances is unique to each individual. I'll reference what I said earlier in the question about cash flow as a resident. The primary role of life insurance is protection. If you are married and have a child, I would recommend that you consider purchasing as much term life insurance as you can afford from a mutual life insurance company that has a conversion feature in the contract. This will allow you to convert to a cash value policy later as an attending while preserving your health rating. When you convert, the premium will be calculated based on your age at the time of conversion, but you will likely preserve the health rating that you got on the term life contract.

~~~~~~~~~~

I have limited funds. If I had to choose between a life insurance contract and a long-term disability contract, which should I get?

A long-term disability is a bigger risk and higher priority because you are still alive, cannot create income, but you are still creating cost through living expenses. Death erases your future earnings, but you are no longer creating costs. Provided you do not have people counting on you, then you are likely best served by investing in the long-term disability contract over the life insurance. A good agent can help you navigate that discussion and decision.

~~~~~~~~~~

How do I choose a financial advisor to work with?

It depends on what you are looking for and what you want them to do for you. A big factor here is compensation. Let's put aside ethics for a moment and assume everyone is ethical. There are bad commission based advisors as well as bad fee based advisors. If you want good long-term support, you need to choose the advisor that is compensated to serve you well long term. Commission based advisors typically receive the bulk of their compensation up front and have little financial incentive to support you in years 2+. Yes, they may receive a servicing fee on the policy, but it will be between 2%-10% of the premium on average. Most people don't cancel contracts because they bought them when they were younger and healthier, so even if they provide poor or no service after the initial sale there is little consequence.

It depends on where you will be in 5-years and whether or not you care about seeing your agent face to face.

If you are in residency and you just want to get a long-term disability contract, choose an advisor that appears knowledgeable about multiple contracts and that can shop across multiple companies.

~~~~~~~~~

What are the biggest mistakes you see new attendings make?

Big house, big cars, and big lifestyle. Then, when they add a spouse and a couple of kids, **they return to being just as broke as they were in residency – except now being broke lasts for the rest of their lives.**

Cash flow management is the single greatest determinant of long-term financial success or financial failure.

Plan your cash flow for housing and cars based upon who you believe you will be in five-years. If you think one of the spouses will want to pull back from work when kids arrive, then base your housing decision on a single income then you'll have that flexibility built into the plan. Once a family commits to a certain lifestyle, it is very difficult to re-engineer and scale back down.

~~~~~~~~~

One of the attending physicians in my hospital introduced me to this guy that can get me into a special real estate investment, part owner in a line of car washes, buy a fast food franchise, etc. Should I do it?

There are too many considerations and variables for me to answer these kinds of questions in a static format like a book or a magazine article, but here are a couple of things for you to consider and discuss with a qualified legal/business professional:

1) Liquidity – do you have the cash available to make this kind of investment?

2) Risk - if you cannot afford to lose your investment, then don't do it.

3) What is your time commitment to the investment?

I had a prospective client that worked 60 hours a week tell me he was about to write a check for $100,000 to purchase a fast food franchise because he figured that he'd just hire a manager and then he'd receive $100,000/year in profits just because he was the owner. If it were that easy, everyone would own a fast food franchise. The reality is that successful restaurants require a lot of handholding and owner attention in the early going (first 5-10 years).

~~~~~~~~~

The idea of working with a financial advisor doesn't appeal to me. Is there a website or an app that I can use that basically does what you do for free?

There are many people out there that prefer to manage their own finances. Smartphone apps like Mint do a really good job helping with cash flow management. There are robot advisors that will manage your investment accounts. You can consider using a website like LegalZoom to help you with your legal needs.

To directly answer the question, is there a website or an APP that you can use that does what I do for my clients? The answer to that is unequivocally no. Sure, there are websites out there that do a lot of the tactical work that falls under the umbrella of financial management. Where they fall short (as of this writing in 2017 and in a pre-artificial intelligence world) is in the being a family sounding board and a financial advocate for the family.

In terms of being a family sounding board, there are lots of times where my clients ask me to help them talk through two competing job offers. Sure, its financially related, but it isn't always 100% about money. The way I serve my clients is to first get to know them as people. What is their vision of the ideal? What scares them? What do they look forward to? What gives them confidence? Once I get to know them as people, then I can help guide them in terms of their money decisions and help them achieve financial balance.

Consider the topic of cash flow management. Cash flow management discussions are often related to behavior management. A perfect analogy to cash flow management is the fitness and weight loss. Are there APPs for smartphones that help people with dieting and fitness? Of course there are, and many of them are free. Well, if they are available, many of them are free, and people desire to be fit and skinny, then why isn't everyone fit and skinny? Conversely, people that work with a personal trainer tend to get better results because it's a human being that takes the time to learn the client and walks alongside them as they move towards their desired objectives.

~~~~~~~~~

I've been told that once I make attending that I should continue to live like a resident for three years and use my surplus cash flow to pay off my school loans. Is that a good idea?

Maybe. Maybe not. There are a wide range of factors to consider. First off, now that you've finally become an attending, are you willing to live like a pauper for another three years? If you can do it, and your loans are such a big headache and causing so much stress, then maybe this is the solution for you.

On the other hand, if you're not overly bothered by the loans and you don't really like the idea of continuing to live like a resident, you could compromise and find a middle ground, putting a little extra towards your loan repayments every month to get them out of the way sooner.

Yet another option is to put that extra cash towards an investment scheme, but only if it earns you more than you're paying in interest on your loans, or you'll be swimming against the current.

The point I'm trying to make is that there are so many variables to consider that it's impossible to answer this question without actually talking to you in person and seeing what your situation is and what your goals are.

QUICK SUMMARY OF ALL ACTION STEPS

SUMMARY FROM PROTECTION MATTERS

In the Protection Matters section, there is an overriding concept called Human Life Value, which is defined as follows:

"That value (Human Life Value) may be defined as the capitalized monetary worth of the earning capacity resulting from the economic forces that are incorporated within our being: namely, our character and health, our education, training, and experience, our personality and industry, our creative power, and or driving force to realize the economic images of the mind."

-Taken from **The Economics of Life Insurance, Third Edition by S.S. Huebner, Page 5**

Your Human Life Value is the lump sum equivalent of all of your future paychecks backing out inflation, taxes and personal consumption. Ideally, you'd like to fully insulate yourself from loss of your own Human Life Value or to be negatively affected by the loss of someone elses Human Life Value.

Here are three areas that you may want to consider the impacts of losing some or all of your future income and taking steps to reduce those impacts through different types of insurance coverage.

☐ **<u>UMBRELLA LIABILITY INSURANCE</u>**: Consider a bad accident that is your fault and the driver in the vehicle you hit is badly injured or worse. If you've taken away their ability to work, there is a possibility that you might be on the hook for a their future income. Speak with an experienced auto insurance and homeowner's insurance agent and ask about Umbrella Liability Insurance.

☐ **<u>LONG-TERM DISABILITY PROTECTION</u>**: You have to protect your unique ability (your specific specialty) because the last thing you want to do is end up being the living dead. You might be tempted to pick up the first insurance policy you find, but you will have to work with a licensed agent that has deep knowledge in this area or you are short-changing yourself. Remember, you get what you pay for, and cutting corners might save you a buck or two in the short-term, but could lead you and your family to financial ruin in the long term. **Find a good agent who is intimately acquainted with and has extensive experience in working with residents and attending and get that protection.**

☐ **<u>LIFE INSURANCE PROTECTION</u>**: Depending on your family situation and whether or not you've gotten someone else to co-sign for loans, you might want to obtain some level of life insurance coverage. If you have a spouse and children, you may want to consider getting life insurance equivalent to your Human Life Value. **There are many different types of life insurance coverage. Have an agent that is experienced in working with physicians explain the different types of coverage and help you protect as much of your future income from loss stemming from premature death as possible.**

SUMMARY FROM CASH FLOW MANAGEMENT

THE GREATEST DETERMINANT BETWEEN FINANCIAL SUCCESS AND FINANCIAL FAILURE IS PROPER CASH FLOW MANAGEMENT

☐ **5-YEARS POST RESIDENCY** - Imagine what you want your life to look like five-years into your career as an attending. Where are you living? Who are you living with? What life changes do you expect will occur during that time? Will you have children? Will you and your partner both continue to work at the same pace and earnings or is it desirable that one or both of you might pull back from work? Consider these questions carefully and decide if it would be prudent to build slack into your budget. The decisions that you make here will have the largest impact on how you choose to spend towards housing (15% of monthly cash flow max) and cars.

☐ **30-SECOND BUDGET** - Build your budget around your expected first-year attending salary while taking into account the things you wrote down in the previous exercise. If you came to the conclusion that you want to build in 10% slack into your budget, then simply add that amount to your savings category such that for the first 5-years you are saving 30%, taxes 30% and lifestyle is 40%. Then, when the lifestyle change occurs, you can simply shift to saving 20%, taxes 30% and lifestyle 50%. Email me at john.crane@ffgadvisors.com for a FREE cash flow spreadsheet that you can use to build, test and measure different cash flow scenarios for yourself.

☐ **<u>STUDENT LOAN MANAGEMENT</u>** - Review your student loans. If they don't make sense to you, call the loan servicing company and ask them to explain them to you. Ask your existing servicing company if they have the ability to reduce your interest rate. Sometimes they will have special programs where they can consolidate your more expensive loans and give you better loan terms. Beware of companies that market to you with loan consolidation programs. Their attractive sounding offer might not be a better deal for you - even if they are offering a lower monthly payment.

SUMMARY FROM NO FREE LUNCH

☐ **<u>CHOOSE AN INVESTMENT PHILOSOPHY</u>** - The stock market most commonly plays a role in most Americans' long-term wealth building in the form of employer-provided retirement accounts. Decide upon an overall investment philosophy and then stick to that philosophy over the long term. For recommended reading on the topic, you may want to look at **A Random Walk Down Wall Street by Burton Makiel**.

☐ **<u>BEHAVIOR MATTERS</u>** - The company DALBAR monitors and tracks actual investor returns. DALBAR's report entitled Annual Quantitative Analysis of Investor Behavior is one of the most commonly referenced documents by investment management companies. In this study, DALBAR compares one of the major stock market indices (the S&P 500) with actual investor returns over a sliding 20-year period. The comparison shows that the unmanaged S&P 500 typically outperforms the average investor during these 20-year periods between 3-5%! The reason for the performance gap is Investor Behavior is typically poor. The average investor will buy and sell their investments at the wrong times. Hold equities for the long term, diversify, rebalance and BEHAVE!

☐ **BE SKEPTICAL AND ASK THE QUESTION** - If this investment opportunity is such a lock for me, then why do you need my money to make it work? Why aren't you mortgaging your house and borrowing money from everyone you know instead of talking to me? When it comes to investing, learn to ask a lot of questions and/or surround yourself with an advisory team that represents your interests and can help you ask those questions.

END NOTES

[i] S.S. Huebner, The Economics of Life Insurance, Third Edition, (Cherry Hill: Executive Asset Management, Inc, 1996), 5.

[ii] Life Happens, "What Your Need to Know About Life Insurance," Page 5, Table A. (http://www.lifehappens.org/wp-content/uploads/2013/10/brochure_LI_WhatYouNeedtoKnowAbout LifeInsurance_Consumer.pdf)

[iii] U.S. Social Security Administration, Fact Sheet February 7, 2013

[iv] Nick Schwartz, "The average career earnings of athletes across America's major sports will shock you," USA Today, October 24, 2013 (http://ftw.usatoday.com/2013/10/average-career-earnings-nfl-nba-mlb-nhl-mls)

[v] Leigh Steinberg, "5 Reasons Why 80% of Retired NFL Players Go Broke," Forbes, Feb 9, 2015 (http://www.forbes.com/sites/leighsteinberg/2015/02/09/5-reasons-why-80-of-retired-nfl-players-go-broke/#2151268e4e36)

[vi] Wikipedia Contributors. "Trinity Study." Wikipedia, The Free Encyclopedia. 8 Mar. 2017. Web 8 Mar. 2017. <https://en.wikipedia.org/wiki/Trinity_study>

Made in the USA
Middletown, DE
06 February 2018